Stone Age Secrets for Mind and Body

Claire Bell

MIDLIFEXPRESS EPUBLISHING

TASMANIA, AUSTRALIA

2014

MIDLIFEXPRESS
PUBLISHED BY MIDLIFEXPRESS EPUBLISHING
MIDLIFEXPRESS.COM
MIDLIFEX@MIDLIFEXPRESS.COM
TASMANIA, AUSTRALIA

SOME OF THIS MATERIAL HAS PREVIOUSLY APPEARED IN
MIDLIFEXPRESS.COM

PRINT ISBN: 978-0-9873128-3-9

Dedication

For my sister, Sue.

I would like to thank my tech-savvy sister Sue Bell for her superb design work. I would also like to thank Pennie Kendall, Heidi Moon and Angie Smales for their useful early-draft suggestions, Suellen Horsley for her contributions to the Retreat chapter and Merridy Pugh for editing the manuscript and allowing me to incorporate her Picnics article into the Nature chapter.

TABLE OF CONTENTS

Introduction   5
Stone Age Secret One - Nature   11
Stone Age Secret Two - Whole Foods   35
Stone Age Secret Three - Art, Craft and Music   70
Stone Age Secret Four - Retreats   81
Stone Age Secret Five - Community   96
Epilogue   105
Resources and References   107

INTRODUCTION

It's not enough to be busy. We must ask: what are we busy about?

~ Henry David Thoreau

Why would anyone want to revisit the Stone Age?

Why would any sane, well-fed, and comfortably housed modern human think he or she would benefit from the wisdom of a long-dead people?

If we think of Stone Age life at all, most of us believe it to have been cold, barbarous, and brutally short for its human inhabitants. I believed this, too, until I delved deeper and researched this era for the better part of a year. What I know now is that, although prehistoric people lived in a fierce world, their lives were not as wretched or brief as I once thought.

Dr Philip J Goscienski, author of *Health Secrets of the Stone Age*, says it's untrue that Stone Age people rarely lived till old age. Indeed, he says, anthropologists have known for decades that 10 percent of Stone Age humans survived to the age of 60 years. The reason we think otherwise is because high infant mortality rates skew the longevity statistics to make it appear prehistoric people were almost all dead by the age of 18.

Stone Age skeletons are strong and sturdy and I suspect the brains their skulls once enshrined were robust as well.

Until recently, we knew little about Stone Age people's lives. Their secrets lay buried under earth and rock for millennia before being exhumed, pieced together, and revealed to us by anthropologists and archaeologists. What they found can help us cope with the frantic pace of modern life in the 21st century.

How this book can help you

My book's premise is that the secret to better mental and physical health lies with our distant ancestors. But I want to be clear at the outset: although I value the virtues of Stone Age life, I want to avoid romanticizing its difficulties – which were many.

We've evolved and adapted to the modern world in a myriad of ways but it's also driving us crazy. Here, for example, are several news items I encountered recently:

- This year (2013), four million Australians will experience mental ill-health. In Australia today, there are more people with depression than there are with a common cold.

- One in seven Australians will suffer an anxiety disorder this year.

- 70 percent of Americans are currently taking prescription drugs. After antibiotics, the most commonly prescribed drug is antidepressants.

- Nearly 1 in 4 American women aged 50–64 are on antidepressants.

- 13 percent of the entire American population is on antidepressants.

- 70 percent of Americans hate their jobs or have 'checked out' of them.

- The suicide rate among Americans aged 35–64 years increased 28.4 percent between 1999 and 2010.

- Loneliness in Western urban society is now at un-precedented levels.

Although these statistics point to a dispirited species, there is a way to meet our troubled world with grace and grit.

And the people of the Stone Age can show us how.

In Chapter One, Nature, I explain how to quiet the mind and soothe the body by heading outside and basking in the natural world like our ancestors once did.

In Chapter Two, Wholefoods, I offer simple, nourishing recipes using (mostly) Stone Age ingredients.

In Chapter Three, I explore prehistoric art, craft, and music-making and suggest why it's a good idea to start one of them now.

Chapter Four, Retreats, explains the benefits of leaving your routine and heading into the unknown to rest, rejuvenate, and gain clarity.

Finally, Chapter Five, Community, digs into the human need for connection and belonging and suggests ways to reclaim our communal past.

Where it all began

This book began as a short article for Midlifexpress, a blog for midlife women my sister and I started way back in 2008. The piece was originally called The

Mesolithic Diet for the Mind (Mesolithic being the scientific word for Middle Stone Age) and was inspired by the Paleolithic diet that encourages people to eat more like their Stone Age forebears for better health.

The Paleolithic diet got me thinking that if there's an optimal Stone Age diet for the body, then perhaps there's an optimal Stone Age diet for the mind. I proceeded to write a lighthearted, fanciful article, not expecting much of a fuss. To my surprise, however, it's been the most popular piece we've published.

I then thought about how I could expand the original idea into a book that is both serious and lighthearted – like the original article.

Soon after, I set about the arduous task of actually writing the thing. Along the way I incorporated Stone Age-inspired recipes we published on Midlifexpress over the years. I thus modified the title to include the word *body*. Hence the book became *The Mesolithic Diet for Mind and Body*.

But almost without exception, everybody hated the title and it had to go.

To cut a long story short, an editor suggested I call it *Stone Age Secrets for Mind and Body*. The rest, as they say, is history. Or prehistory in this case.

Stone Age Secret One
Nature

I once read of an exercise program for the elderly where therapists took people to neighbourhood parks and taught them to stretch. What got my attention was a woman who said she'd lived in the area for 10 years and had never visited any of her local greenery. Incredible. Other people said it was good to breathe fresh air and how little they had done so until the program began.

Our Stone Age ancestors would find this unthinkable because they were always outside. But not us. We live mostly indoors, cocooned in temperate habitats that bear little resemblance to the exterior world. Cave trolls thrive in this environment, but we're creatures of the sun and need plenty of time outside. And why wait until we're old and stiff and for someone else to organize it for us?

Here are four simple ways to reclaim our outdoor Stone Age spirit.

WALKING

Everywhere is walking distance if you have the time.

~ Steven Wright

These days we know a lot about the body and how it works. We certainly know more about its anatomy and physiology than did our prehistoric forebears. Scientific experiments consistently find that our physical and mental wellbeing improves when we get off the couch and exercise. Yet millions of us are fat and depressed and riddled with chronic health problems.

Walking's a fine way to temper sloth and melancholy

and Stone Age people must have felt upbeat most
of the time because they walked everywhere. I like
walking because it feels good and it resists my urge to
rush.

Here's what science knows about walking:

- It's a low-impact exercise that puts minimal stress
  on muscles and joints;
- It reduces the need for medication. Researchers
  from The National Walkers' Health Study, which
  comprised 32,000 women and 8,000 men, found
  those who took the longest weekly walks took less
  medications;
- It confers longer breast cancer survival. Women
  who walk regularly after being diagnosed with
  breast cancer have a 45 per cent greater chance
  of survival than those who are inactive, according
  to a study published in the Journal of Clinical
  Oncology;
- It lessens stroke risk - as long as people do a brisk
  30 minute walk, five days a week;
- It builds bones because walking requires that we
  carry our own body weight;
- It reduces heart disease risk;
- It improves blood pressure and blood sugar levels;
- It stabilises body weight;
- It lowers breast and colon cancer risk;
- It cuts the prospect of non-insulin dependent
  (Type 2) diabetes;
- It improves mood; and
- It increases oxytocin levels. This is very, very good.

Oxytocin interpolation

Oxytocin is known as the pleasure hormone, the trust hormone and the love hormone. Whatever its name, I love it. And so should you. It builds trust, inspires generosity, strengthens social relations and heals wounds because it's anti-inflammatory. It also makes us more optimistic, less depressed and generally better to be around.

Additionally, oxytocin lowers blood cortisol levels. Cortisol is the stress hormone. It causes inflammation, which is bad for our body.

We produce oxytocin when we exercise, hug each other, gaze at someone we like, give birth, shake hands and do something thrilling.

To boost oxytocin, go for a walk; hug a dog or cat because stroking and hugging a pet increases our oxytocin levels (and theirs too). Hug friends and family. Eight hugs a day gets our oxytocin levels flowing and our health improving.

What artists and poets and philosophers know about walking

- Walking develops independence and confidence because we rely on our own body to get somewhere.
- Walking invites adventure because it allows us access to places unreachable by car. A shaman once took a group of us into a forest that ran alongside a busy road. We rambled over fallen trees and through dense vegetation until we reached a beautiful grove that reminded me of Rivendell, the

elf city in Lord of the Rings. The shaman told us few people knew this place existed even though it was next to a large town. I remember thinking how glad I was that cars were unable to ruin it.

All truly great thoughts are conceived by walking.

~ Friedrich Nietzsche

She walks in beauty, like the night. Of countless climbs and starry skies…

~ Lord Byron

Creative walking

I will rise now, and go about the city in the streets, and in the broad ways I will seek him whom my soul loveth.

~ Song of Solomon 3:2

I like to vary the style, length, and velocity of my walks. It keeps me interested. Here are a few suggestions.

The stroll: This genial locomotion consists of a leisurely walk in whatever direction appeals. It was popular with pre-revolutionary French royalty, Jane Austen's more thoughtful and elegant characters, Egyptian pharaohs, Roman emperors and Renaissance poets.

These days, however, the stroll's languid pace is best suited to close friends or lovers because of its unhurried and meditative character. Good friends are comfortable with contemplative moments and feel little need to disrupt the silence with inane or nervous chatter.

Lovers benefit because the stroll's languor calms a frantic heart and soothes a feverish mind.

Strolling is not recommended if accompanied by feisty dogs, peevish toddlers, unruly mobs, or Type A personalities.

Take a walk on the wild side.

~ Lou Reed

The prowl: This prehistoric peregrination has a bloodthirsty history and our Stone Age ancestors were its biggest fans. As a 21st century walking style, however, it has a place provided it's used cautiously. Contemporary prowling is best done outdoors at farmers' markets or indoors in supermarket aisles. The prowl requires stealth, cunning and sudden bursts of speed as its practitioner prepares to pounce on unsuspecting produce.

Prowling is best done alone. Fellow prowlers are distracting, untrustworthy and ill-mannered. What's more, they're notorious for separating us from our hard-won bounty and devouring it themselves.

I like long walks, especially when they are taken by people *who annoy me.*

~ Noel Coward

The Nordic ski walk: This odd-looking jaunt provides a whole body workout. It needs two specially designed rubber-tipped poles which are swung in unison with its proponent's steps. It can be used in all seasons and in all climates. (Stone Age people probably improvised with tree branches, spears, and bamboo.) It's especially good for those who hunch over computers because it loosens the shoulders and disinhibits the neck. It also improves balance and helps people with knee or leg problems because the poles provide stability. It's an excellent cardio workout because it fires up the heart.

You've gotta stay in shape. My grandma started walking five miles a day when she was sixty. She's ninety-seven now and we don't know where the heck she is.

~ Ellen DeGeneres

The Enid Blyton ramble: This free-spirited gait has fallen into such disfavour of late that it's practically extinct. Workaholics accuse ramblers of irrelevance because they add little to economic growth and do nothing to expand Gross Domestic Product. In this sense, engaging in a ramble is counter-cultural and eco-friendly in the extreme, and all the more reason to do so. It's suited to forest hikes with favourite cousins, eccentric aunts, children's authors, and unhinged scientists. The ramble appeals to rebels, artists, spiritual teachers, and creative types of all persuasions. This is because its aimlessness relaxes the thinking mind and frees it to reflect upon life's great mysteries.

Canines – particularly Labradors, Golden Retrievers, and Border Collies – also appreciate the potential of a good, uninhibited ramble.

If I could not walk far and fast, I think I should just explode and perish.

~ Charles Dickens

The stride: This exertive move was popular with Stone Age warriors, medieval knights, and 19th century explorers. Its lusty style requires long, intrepid steps done with a purposeful sense of destination. The stride boosts confidence, exudes authority, and provides plenty of air for the lungs and a fine workout for the heart.

Low level warning: Although striding is admirable it can appear egotistical. As such, it may intimidate some and infuriate others and is best done alone across an empty football field or in public before a vast, adoring crowd. People uncomfortable with attention or who lack a modicum of fitness will struggle to keep up. If people insist on performing this style with friends, they must ensure their First Aid training is current and their accomplices' egos are healthy.

The stride is excellent if accompanied by a faithful canine, a bunch of jovial Hobbits, or a self-possessed, physically fit, and extroverted friend.

I shall wear white flannel trousers and walk along the beach.

~ T S Eliot, *The Love Song of J Alfred Prufrock*

The waddle: This comedic constitutional requires a hobbling step. It's good for a laugh and laughter fortifies the heart and lungs, releases endorphins, and improves mental health. Waddling is best done after a feast, at a lakeside picnic, or late at night when the mood mellows and expectations are low.

I learnt to walk as a baby and I haven't had a lesson since.

~ Marilyn Monroe

The strut: This peacock-like progression is more egotistical than the stride and is best done away from crowds as it will provoke egg-throwing and bellicose laughter. It requires a proud and lofty manner coupled with a strong desire to impress. It's suited to great personal victory but may appear vapid and vainglorious if overdone. Nevertheless, this walking style is perfect to mark triumph as long as one is careful with location.

Therefore, it's best to strut in a sheltered grove, on a deserted beach, or on an open air stage before the crowds arrive. It's wise to revert to a more humble locomotive style when an audience materialises.

You cannot teach a crab to walk straight.

~ Aristophanes

The silly walk: Comedian John Cleese – in his Monty Python incarnation – perfected a walk so idiotic it remains unrivalled to this day. Silly walks are best done after a long night partying when people are ready for a laugh and too inebriated or exhausted to seek professional entertainment.

The skulk: This ancient walk is a less sinister and more socially acceptable version of the prowl. Nevertheless, like its Stone Age cousin, it needs to be used with care. The skulk requires a discreet, semi-benign slink, preferably behind bushes, and it works well when its proponent wishes to remain unnoticed. As such, it's best done alone or with a companion who also wants anonymity. It's unwise to skulk with children, royalty, dogs, and celebrities. All four require reassurance and attention and this primordial pace calls for committed inconspicuousness.

If you don't know how to do it, I'll show you how to walk the dog.

~ The Rolling Stones

The somnambulation: Sleepwalking is cheap and eco-friendly and it's a great way to rest and exercise simultaneously. Stone Age somnambulists slept in the open or in habitats with plenty of ventilation.

This encouraged good health but meant death if they somnambulated too near a cave lion.

Death also stalks contemporary somnambulists if they live in high-rise apartments or near busy roads. This walking style is best done alone because its odd body movements, sporadic drooling, and strange vocalisations, combine to unnerve even the most enthusiastic of companions.

A pedestrian is a man in danger of his life. A walker is a man in possession of his soul.

~ David McCord

The parade: This style is best done in a parade, but it comes in handy as a general confidence booster if its proponent marches purposefully about as if in a procession. It's preferably practised alone – unless, of course, there's a parade to join. Unsuitable for close friends (unless they hail from a military or circus background), skittish dogs, and enochlophobics*. It's particularly popular with children, B Grade celebrities in search of A Grade status, and brass bands.

* Enochlophobics dread crowds and with good reason. Large human congregations have a tendency to turn perverse and, as such, a crowd-attendee's risk of death by trampling, viral infection, existential angst and as-phyxiation is ever-present.

With beauty before me, may I walk
With beauty behind me, may I walk
With beauty above me, may I walk
With beauty below me, may I walk
With beauty all around me, may I walk
Wandering on the trail of beauty, may I walk.

~ A Navajo Walking Meditation

The meander: This delightful creature comes to us from the Greek word Maiandos, the name of a winding river in Caria. Despite its sweet name, however, this walk flounders in the modern world because it requires its proponents to wind their way around forests, meadows, woods and fields in a wistful and meditative manner. Its sheer aimlessness dismays hard-line economists in the same way a good ramble does. Although it was popular with druids, medieval wizards and forest-dwelling Christian saints it has since fallen into disuse. The meander is excellent with small-to-medium size groups and is especially suited to those seeking insight and creativity. Children enjoy the meander as do elderly relatives, romantic poets, and old-school schoolteachers.*

*Pedagogues, particularly the old-time British schoolmaster, concocted creative teaching ideas after meandering in the fields and forests adjacent to their learning institutions. Please refer to the movies *Goodbye Mr Chips* and *Dead Poets' Society* for further insight.

They walked through the rainy dark like gaunt ghosts, and Garraty didn't like to look at them. They were the walking dead.

~ Stephen King, *The Long Walk*

The lurch: The lurch is a necessary addition to the walking pantheon because it coincides with today's zombie zeitgeist. I practise it every so often in preparation for joining the undead battalions or for a role in the latest zombie flick.

Lurching requires a lumbering stride while the upper body is thrust forward in awkward, jerky movements. It can be done alone but is more realistic if done with a group.

So there you have it. Pick a style and stagger into the fray.

EARTHING

I sing the body electric.

~ Walt Whitman, *Leaves of Grass*

A few years ago I read *Earthing*, by Clinton Ober, Martin Zucker, and Stephen T Sinatra MD, and learned we're all electron deficient. The culprits are

shoes, sleeping above the floor, and working indoors because they separate us from the subtle electrical currents our planet generates. Stone Age people, however, were electron abundant because they earthed continuously. They wore rudimentary footwear, slept on the ground, and worked outdoors.

When we earth, we place our bare feet on the ground and our bodies become suffused with negatively charged free electrons. This leads to a warm, tingling sensation and feelings of ease and wellbeing. Earthing's good for us because it:

- alleviates or eliminates symptoms of many inflammatory diseases;
- reduces or banishes chronic pain;
- improves sleep;
- increases energy;
- soothes and calms body and mind;

- normalises body rhythms;
- thins blood and improves blood pressure and flow; and
- protects the body from potentially health disturbing environmental electromagnetic fields (EMFs).

The Chinese and Indians were on to all this thousands of years ago, of course. They both have their own word for earthing. The Chinese call it Qi (pronounced chee) and it's regarded as the energy or natural force that permeates the universe. India's Vedic tradition calls this primordial energy Prana, which means 'vital force'.

A natural gait is biomechanically impossible for any shoe-wearing person.

~ Dr William Rossi, Podiatrist

Shoes are great separators and one of the best ways to earth is to ditch our shoes for as long as possible each day.

I wear shoes infrequently. Here's what I've noticed:

- My toes breathe and the spaces between them have widened;
- My feet have grown half a shoe size. I've either been wearing the wrong size or my feet are expanding into freedom;
- I like my feet now;
- When I put shoes on I want to take them straight off;
- My bunions have reduced and my blisters have gone. I'd had bunions for years;
- When I do buy shoes I ensure I can spread my toes

wide apart in them. Anything else means cramp and constriction; and
- My feet are warm – they were nearly always cold.

So go Stone Age and wean yourself off the shoe habit.

Get to know your feet.

Stretch the toes apart with your fingers.

Wriggle and gently tug each toe.

Massage the feet with fragrant oils.

Pick up marbles with each toe so they regain a sense of working individually.

Interlace your fingers between your toes and spread your fingers wide.

Here's another good reason to go shoeless: shoe wearing atrophies the part of the brain that receives sensory input from our feet.

Dr Michael Merzenich is a neuroscientist and professor emeritus at the University of California in San Francisco. He's also a neuroplasticity expert. Neuroplasticity contends that the brain, rather than being fixed and unchanging, is malleable and able to alter its structure and function well into old age.

Dr Merzenich says shoe-wearing reduces the feedback from our feet to our brain and we need to go shoeless on a variety of surfaces to prevent the brain's feet-sensing map from atrophying.

PICNICKING

The Stone Age was no picnic for its inhabitants, but picnicking for us is a marvelous way to revisit the prehistoric eating experience.

A picnic, like walking and earthing, propels us into the fresh air and sunlight, connects us with people, and provides a healthy nutritional encounter.

Picnicking was popular throughout history, although it suffered a minor setback with the release of *Picnic at Hanging Rock* in 1975. This spine-withering flick is one of Australia's most popular, successful, and spooky movies. It's based on the 1967 novel by Joan Lindsay, who scared her already petrified readers witless by refusing to reveal whether it was fact or fiction. This led most Australians, including me, to concur her book was based on a true story.

This misapprehension was partly our fault, but Ms Lindsay also bears some responsibility.
This is because she wrote: 'Whether picnic at Hanging Rock is fact or fiction, my readers must decide for themselves. As the fateful picnic took place in the year nineteen hundred…' etc., etc.

Most of us decided it was true.

In any case, we were willingly duped because the facts are easily checkable.

Here's how I learned The Truth: My mother and sister went to the library to read press clippings from the time. When they asked for the relevant newspaper coverage, the librarian smiled and told them:

a) There was no St Valentine's Day school picnic at Hanging Rock in 1900.

b) There were no press clippings because nothing had happened.

c) When pressed by journalists as to why she hinted her tale was factual, Ms Lindsay simply said it was true for her. (Who knows if Joan really said that, but librarians are benign and reliable people so she probably did.) In any case, true or false, the book and movie were huge hits and terrified the intestinal contents out of everyone.

Here's why: On St. Valentine's Day, 1900, a group of schoolgirls and two of their teachers head off for a picnic at a geological rock formation called Hanging Rock. (This place does exist and it's about two hours' drive from my place. I've been there. Nothing happened.)

Lots of bone-liquefying panpipe music, high-pitched screaming, and ethereal camera work later, several of the girls and one of their teachers disappear, never to be seen again.

Witnesses go mad, the headmistress hangs herself, and no one is ever the same again.

Apart from this supernatural dining al fresco calamity, however, the picnic is still a much loved and thoroughly commendable Stone Age outdoor eating tradition designed to calm the nerves and fortify the spirit.

The virtues of a good picnic

Writer Merridy Pugh extols the virtues of a good picnic:

Eating out has become such a ubiquitous pastime in Aussie culture that perhaps we overlook that simplest of eating out occasions – the picnic. By 'eating out' I mean the custom of eating at restaurants – including the coffee-café craze and the frenzy of fast food outlets.

But a meal 'out' can be just that. Out of the house. Out of doors. Out of the rat race.

A pleasure excursion

A quick googling of 'picnic' throws up a swathe of

similar sounding definitions:

An outing or occasion that involves taking a packed meal to be eaten outdoors.

A meal eaten outdoors, as on an excursion.

An excursion or outing with food usually provided by members of the group and eaten in the open.

And my favourite (thanks, Wikipedia!)... *A picnic is a pleasure excursion at which a meal is eaten outdoors (al fresco or en plein air), ideally taking place in a beautiful landscape such as a park, beside a lake...* Descriptions of picnics show that the idea of a meal that was jointly contributed to and was enjoyed out-of-doors were essential to a picnic from the early 19th century.

I like this last description because it indicates that the primary purpose of a picnic is the *communal enjoyment of food in a setting of natural beauty.* (Ed. Note. How much more Stone Age can it get?)

Simplicity

Part of the charm of picnicking lies in its simplicity. Preparation can be elaborate but needn't be. One can picnic in the back garden with a sandwich.
And a picnic's delights are simple delights: food, fresh air, conversation.

Solitary or shared

Communal picnicking in a delightful setting promotes good feeling and shared pleasure. Exercise can be an adjunct to the meal – walking to the picnic spot, or playing an outdoor game. There are other advantages: you can take your dog to a picnic.

Picnicking together allows communication to unfold in a way that restaurants do not – one is not confined to a particular seat with particular neighbours; conversation is unhindered by background noise or loud music. Cutlery may be dispensed with and an air of relaxation prevails.

And of course solitary picnics hold their own charms. A solitary picnic promotes silent contemplation and quiet appreciation. It's a hiatus in the normal run of events. It requires nothing more than the simplest of packed foods and a spot of reasonable weather.

Whether the weather

Being subject to the vagaries of weather is equally the picnicker's delight, frustration, excitement or disaster. I've watched picnickers huddling vainly under sodden umbrellas. I've been one of them. A picnic in fine weather is heaven; a picnic in gale force winds can be purgatory. Either way, one must be prepared for the elements.

But isn't a barbie a picnic?

It depends.

Barbecues add the element of cooking. Communal cooking round the barbie is a wonderful icebreaker, and usually people bring food to share.

Barbecuing is traditionally done outdoors, though eating outside isn't always a natural consequence. But take your sausages to a barbie in a park – yes, that's picnicking!

Peculiar picnic facts

1. The word piquenique first appeared in print in 1692, referring to a group of diners in a restaurant who brought their own wine (Tony Willis, Origines de la Langue Française).

2. After the French Revolution in 1789 royal parks opened to the public for the first time. Picnicking in the parks became popular among newly enfranchised citizens.

3. In 1989 the Pan-European Picnic was held on both sides of the Austrian-Hungarian border. It was a political statement in the campaign for German reunification.

4. In 2000 a 600-mile long picnic spanned the length of France. It marked the first Bastille Day of the New Millennium.

5. The Northern Territory has a public holiday called Picnic Day.

CLOUD SPOTTING

*And so we say to all who'll listen: Look up, marvel at
the ephemeral beauty, and live life with your head in the
clouds.*

~ From The Cloud Appreciation Society's Manifesto

Cloud watching is quintessentially Stone Age. It's done
mostly outdoors, is cheap and uplifting and is the ideal
accompaniment to walking, earthing, and picnicking.
It excites rebels, alchemists, and artists alike with its
counter-cultural ethos and opportunity for creative
thought.

But beware, its lack of profit advantage causes
economists to retch and politicians to convulse.
Corporate CEOs, workaholics, and sweatshop
proprietors also detest cloud gazing because it distracts
workers and lowers productivity.

Clouds are patron gods of idle fellows.

~ Aristophanies

This primordial pastime is the perfect antidote to busyness. It raises our gaze from screen to sky and decouples us, at least temporarily, from technology. I remember how sweet it was as a child to look up at the clouds and marvel at their mystery and beauty. I loved to watch their moods and the way they moved and shape-shifted and coalesced into people and mythical beasts.

Dispense with psychoanalysis

Cloud watching saves on psychoanalysis bills because they're nature's version of ink blots, says Gavin Pretor-Pinney, the founder of Britain's Cloud Appreciation Society. He refers to the Rorschach test of the 1960s where people were shown inkblots and their responses recorded in an effort to detect underlying thought disorders. Cloud watching, however, is a much cheaper way to access the unconscious and to reveal hidden meaning.

Clouds are nothing to moan about, says Gavin, but moan we do. If someone's upset we say there's a 'dark cloud' hovering over them. If events look bleak we say there are 'clouds on the horizon'. Clouds are seen as obstructions to happiness and he set up his cloud society to defend clouds from this bad press.

Cloud spotting sanctions doing nothing and keeps us grounded by slowing us down and allowing our minds to play. Clouds are meditative, poetic creations and they're freely available to anyone who looks skyward.

Daydream, give yourself a rest from your thinking mind. Make connections, come up with creative solutions, and connect with the vast universe above.

If you live with your head in the clouds every now and then it helps you keep your feet on the ground.

~ Gavin Pretor-Pinney

Here's some of the more unusual clouds you might like to look out for:

Lenticular: These freakish clouds look like UFOs and are created by gravity waves.

Kelvin-Helmholz waves: Resemble a row of crashing waves.

Notilucent: These mysterious creatures glow at night, hence they're also known as 'night shining' clouds. Notilucent clouds are usually found over the poles but recently they've migrated farther south. They form at lower altitudes than they once did and they're brighter and more numerous, possibly due to climate change.

Tubular: These clouds, also called Morning Glory clouds, can extend 600 kilometres across the sky. They appear every autumn over Burketown, Qld, a remote Australian hamlet with only 200 residents.

WE NEED NATURE TO STAY SANE

Stone Age people had a simpler, less noisy world to deal with. Sure, their lives were tough. No one denies that. But they lived on a sparsely populated planet with clean air and food, and never suffered the misery of traffic jams, supermarkets, political debates, and 24-hour news.

Spiritual teacher Eckhart Tolle says we need nature for our physical survival as well as for our mental health because it takes us out of our heads and into stillness.

A walk, a picnic, a cloud spotting afternoon – all these things invite us to be still, to quiet the voice in our heads and to simply be. Spending time in nature counters busyness and invites us to go within.

Nature is always there for us. It was there in the Stone Age and it's still here now. Make sure you experience it as much as possible every day.

Stone Age Secret Two
Whole Foods

Eat food. Not too much. Mostly plants.

~ Michael Pollan

Stone Age people were opportunists and anything edible was fair game. Their diet comprised herbs, coarse vegetables, plant roots, nuts, eggs, fish, meat, honey, fresh fruit, and berries. They also ate carbohydrates which may surprise those who think these cellulosic compounds played no part in the Stone Age kitchen.

They were definitely present in their diets because traces of seeds from aquatic plants and wild grasses have been unearthed in flooded settlements from the Paleolithic and Mesolithic periods.

Although we have little precise evidence of the type, quality, and quantity of the Stone Age diet, we can be reasonably sure it was:
- seasonal
- fresh
- varied
- colourful
- free from pesticides, herbicides, and industrial chemicals
- cooked simply
- devoid of refined sugar, trans fats, and excess salt
- unprocessed
- locally sourced and prepared
- high in micronutrients, fibre, vitamins, and minerals
- mostly plant-based.

In contrast, modern food is highly processed, unseasonal, sourced globally, and bereft of micronutrients. It's also clobbered with a formidable artillery of fungicides, pesticides and herbicides, many of which threaten to liquefy our internal organs, defoliate what's left of Earth's greenery, and decimate a good proportion of carbon-based life.

I've always suspected this noxious apothecary harms human health and a recent experiment – by a 13-year-old high school student no less – proves organic food is, indeed, much better for us than its chemically enhanced alternative.

Ria Chhaba regularly heard her parents debate whether organic food was better than conventionally grown food and she decided to find out who was right. She experimented with fruit flies to determine whether food grown without chemicals is healthier and for her efforts she was awarded top honours in a national science competition and her results were published in a scientific journal.

Under the auspices of Dr Johannes Bauer, an assistant professor at Southern Methodist University in Dallas, Texas, she found that fruit flies fed an organic diet were healthier, less stressed, more fertile and lived longer than fruit flies fed with conventionally grown produce. Dr Bauer speculates that the flies fed organic produce fared better because they had to deal with less pesticide and fungicide residue in their food.

Stone Age people, of course, never had to contend with chemical food additives. Nor did they overwork their kidneys with excess salt or perforate their pancreases with a surfeit of sugar. They ate locally and seasonally.

The following recipe compendium makes no claim to prehistoric culinary accuracy. I'd call it more of a light-hearted, Stone Age-inspired assemblage as it's vegetarian (because I am) – and we know prehistoric people ate meat whenever they could – and it does include a little butter, cream, and oil. Nevertheless, it's plant-based, uses a variety of foods we know Stone Age people ate and is, at heart, simple, nourishing, and flavoursome.

Most of the recipes are super easy and need minimal equipment, preparation and cooking time. I've divided them into savoury and sweet, with the savoury outweighing the sweet by about five to one. This is deliberate. Stone Age confectionary consisted of fresh fruit and berries and a little honey. Dessert as a serious, emotionally satisfying and tooth-demolishing concern was thousands of years in the future.

ROOT VEGETABLES

You will notice a prevalence of root vegetables in many recipes. This is because they were a basic component of the Stone Age diet. The root vegetable pantheon includes beetroot, parsnip, potato, sweet potato, carrots, radish, swede (also known as rutabaga), and turnip. They're a generous bunch too – full of fibre and slow-digesting carbohydrates – and they have loads of vitamins, including B, A, and C, and minerals including potassium, iron, and zinc.

To recreate the most authentic prehistoric dining experience possible, ensure all your root vegetables are fresh, firm and organic.

Roast potatoes with pine nuts and turmeric

This dish is a superb combination of flavour and crunch. It goes well with salads and vegetable stews. It was particularly popular with prehistoric rodents and giant ground-dwelling sloths.

Preheat oven to 190 Celsius (375 Fahrenheit).

Ingredients
6 medium potatoes, cubed and chopped
80 grams pine nuts
3 tablespoons olive oil
1 teaspoon powdered turmeric or 2 teaspoons grated fresh turmeric
3 cloves garlic, unpeeled
A pinch sea salt (optional)

Next
Place oil in the base of a medium-sized glass or ceramic baking dish. Add turmeric and salt to the oil and mix well.

Add potatoes, pine nuts, and garlic cloves and toss them about jauntily until they are well covered in the oil and turmeric mix.

Place the baking dish in the hot oven and bake for 25 minutes.
Remove from oven and turn the mixture over. Return to oven and cook for another 30 minutes, or until potatoes are soft.

Serves 4.

Roast root vegetables with fresh herbs and paprika

Preheat oven to 200 Celsius (390 Fahrenheit).
It's fine to use any type of root vegetable for this medley.
Here's my favourite combination.

Ingredients
2 large carrots, unpeeled, washed, and cut into large cubes
1 large sweet potato, peeled, and cut into medium cubes
2 white potatoes (can be left unpeeled if organic), washed well and cut into medium-size cubes
1 large, raw beetroot, washed well, unpeeled, and cut into wedges
I parsnip (unpeeled), cut into cubes
1 large red onion, peeled and chopped into small cubes
6 cloves garlic, unpeeled
2 or 3 tablespoons extra virgin olive oil
½ cup water
1 tablespoon sweet paprika
½ teaspoon sea salt (optional)
5 drops tabasco sauce (optional)

Any combination of fresh herbs and as much as you fancy. I'd suggest you start with a small handful of basil, a handful of fresh flat-leaf parsley, and a few tablespoons each of fresh oregano and thyme.

Next

Place olive oil, paprika, tabasco sauce, and water into a large glass or ceramic baking dish. Mix well. Throw in vegetables and herbs and jubilantly toss everything together to ensure they're nicely coated in the oil, water, paprika and optional salt and tabasco sauce.

Bake in the oven for about 30 minutes. Remove from oven and turn over the vegetables. Return to the oven and cook for another 20 to 30 minutes or until the vegetables are soft and aromatic.

Serves 4–6.

Zucchini (pretending to be pasta) with spicy tomato and spinach sauce

While we suspect Stone Age people ate many things, pasta was definitely not one of them. So, here's a fantastic pasta alternative using zucchinis peeled into strips. Grab a vegetable peeler and peel each zucchini lengthwise until you reach the seeds. You'll end up with zucchini strips which you treat just as you would pasta. That is, they're layered in a serving bowl and the pasta sauce is poured over them. Magnificent.

Ingredients
4 large zucchini
1 onion, chopped
8 roma tomatoes
4 cups fresh baby spinach, washed and roughly
chopped
1 cup passata (Italian cooking sauce)
I teaspoon fresh chilli
2 cloves garlic, peeled and crushed or chopped
2 tablespoons olive oil
Fresh herbs to taste. For example, oregano, thyme,
parsley.
½ teaspoon sea salt

Next
Using a vegetable peeler, peel the zucchinis from top to
bottom to get nice long strips. Stop peeling strips when
you get to the seeds.
Heat the oil and ¼ teaspoon salt in a large frying pan.
Add the zucchini strips. They will reduce in size and
volume so don't panic if your pan looks crowded at first.
Toss them gently around until they're evenly coated
with oil and salt. Cover and reduce heat to low and let
the zucchini cook gently until soft, like pasta. On no
account let them turn into mush. Check frequently to
ensure they don't burn. Add a little water if they look
too dry.

Sauce
Chop onion finely and the tomatoes roughly. Place
them in a large saucepan with the passata. Add the
chopped spinach, garlic, fresh herbs and chilli. Bring to
the boil. Reduce heat and simmer for about 20 minutes.
Add salt to taste if you feel the need.
Remove zucchini from pan and distribute evenly into
4 bowls. Pour sauce over each and serve topped with
fresh parsley.

Serves 4.

Lentil and spinach dahl

Lentil remains have been found at Stone Age campsites.
Just as well, because this dish is superb.

Ingredients
2 cans brown lentils, drained
I medium onion, finely chopped
I cup red lentils
3 cups water
400 ml can coconut milk (organic if possible)
3 handfuls of baby spinach, chopped roughly
2 generous tablespoons of good quality plain yoghurt
2 vegetarian stock cubes
1 heaped teaspoon paprika
A handful of roughly chopped parsley

Next

Throw everything into a large saucepan, bring to the
boil and then reduce the heat and simmer until the
red lentils are cooked. This takes about 25 minutes, but
it varies a little. Make sure you stir the pot every five
minutes or so as red lentils have a tendency to stick to
the bottom of almost anything.

Add more water if things start to look like the Sahara
desert.

Add more salt if you want.

I like this dhal to be more of a soup consistency. If you
prefer a drier comestible, however, add less water.

Vegetarian lasagne (gluten free)

This delicious lasagne also uses the versatile zucchini to replace the pasta and the zucchini layer functions in exactly the same way as a layer of traditional lasagne sheets.

Ingredients
5 large zucchini, washed and cut lengthwise into 2cm wide strips
500 grams pumpkin, peeled and roughly chopped
8 large tomatoes, chopped
2 cans brown lentils, drained
2 onions, chopped finely
4 cloves garlic, peeled and grated
3 carrots, grated
2 cups passata or 1 can tomato puree
3 cups water
250 grams ready-made basil pesto (from deli or supermarket)
2 vegetarian low salt stock cubes
Salt and pepper to taste

Next
Preheat oven to 200 Celsius (390 Fahrenheit).
Sprinkle the zucchini strips with a little salt and place them in a lightly greased baking tray in a single layer. Bake for about 20 minutes. Remove from oven and place on a plate ready to use as lasagne layers.

Place chopped pumpkin in a steamer and cook until tender. Mash and add a little freshly ground black pepper. Set aside while you make the vegetable sauce. In a large saucepan gently fry onion and garlic until soft.
Add chopped tomatoes, lentils, grated carrot, passata or

tomato puree, water and stock cubes.
Bring to the boil and simmer for about 15 minutes.

Grab a large baking dish and place half the cooked vegetable sauce over the base.
Place a layer of zucchini over the sauce and spread it with the pesto mix.
Spread the mashed pumpkin evenly over the pesto layer.
Place another layer of zucchini slices over the pumpkin layer.
Place the remaining vegetable sauce over the top.

Cook on middle shelf of oven for about 50 minutes.

Serves 4.

Hearty Stone Age shakshouka

Here's my interpretation of this balmy brimstone of a dish. It consists of poached eggs served in a fiery sauce of tomatoes, cumin, chilli peppers, onion, and spices. It is wonderful as a main meal served with a crisp green salad and it gleefully complements the pumpkin, cauliflower and coriander salmagondis.

Ingredients
4 eggs
4 tomatoes, roughly chopped
1 onion, peeled and finely chopped
2 or 3 cloves garlic, peeled and roughly chopped
1 red capsicum, chopped finely
I tablespoon tomato paste – not Stone Age, but who cares?
1 fresh chilli, chopped
2 teaspoons sweet paprika
1 teaspoon cumin powder
1 cup water
¼ teaspoon salt
A handful of fresh parsley, chopped

Next
Place all the ingredients in a large frying pan and bring to the boil. Reduce heat and simmer for about 20 minutes. Crack the eggs into the sauce. Cover and cook on a low heat for about 10 minutes. If you want a runnier yolk, you may need to check how everything's going after about 6 or 7 minutes.

When the eggs are cooked to your satisfaction, remove pan from heat and place 1 or 2 eggs on a plate.
Spoon sauce over the eggs and garnish with fresh parsley.
This quantity will serve 2 people if they have 2 eggs each or 4 people if only 1 egg each is desired.

Potato and chickpea curry

Yes, chickpeas, like lentils, were around in the Stone Age. Just not in cans. Lucky us.

Ingredients

3 large potatoes, peeled, washed and cut into small cubes
2 large carrots, sliced thinly
1 onion, chopped finely
4 cloves garlic, peeled and chopped
1 can chickpeas
1 can brown lentils
1 bunch coriander, roughly chopped and well washed
2 low salt vegetable stock cubes
Approximately 4 to 5 cups of water – just enough to cover the vegetables
3 tablespoons creamy plain yoghurt – Greek style is best, preferably organic. Please note – this dairy product is optional due to its complete lack of Stone Age credibility.
1 tablespoon tomato paste
1 heaped teaspoon curry powder

Next

Place all the ingredients in a large pot, stir well and bring to the boil. Simmer gently until the vegetables are soft. This will take about 35 minutes. Garnish with fresh coriander.

This hearty dish will serve at least 4 people.

Angie's pumpkin potpourri

Preheat oven to 190 Celsius (375 Farenheit).

Ingredients
500 grams of vegetables such as pumpkin, potato, carrot, or sweet potato, chopped into bite-size pieces
1 onion, chopped roughly
2 cloves garlic, peeled and chopped
Handful of fresh peas or beans to throw over the top
Handful of toasted sesame seeds or pine nuts

Next
Toss the whole lot in an oven proof vessel such as a cast iron baking dish with a lid and a little olive oil infused with rosemary or garlic or chilli.

Top with a handful or two of green vegies.

Cook in the oven until vegetables are soft. The cooking time will depend on the size of your pieces.

Top with a handful or two of toasted sesame seeds or pine nuts.

Serves 3.

Pumpkin, cauliflower, and coriander salmagondis

Salmagondis is a fancy French word for a hodgepodge of wildly disparate things.

This delightful orange miscellany could happily call itself a soup – it all depends on how much water boils off. If you go away and forget it for a while, it will morph into a dhal. If cooked less it's a chirpy soup.

Ingredients

1 small cauliflower (or ½ large cauliflower), washed and broken into medium-size florets
Approximately 500 grams pumpkin, peeled and cubed
2 low salt vegetable stock cubes
About 3 cups water
1 bunch fresh coriander, washed well and chopped. Vietnamese mint is a nice alternative if you have no coriander.
1 teaspoon freshly grated ginger

Next

Place the cauliflower, pumpkin, water, stock cubes, fresh ginger, and half the coriander in a large pot. Bring to the boil, then turn down the heat and simmer, covered, until the vegetables are soft. Lift the lid occasionally to see if you have enough water and that the mixture is not running dry. Then, when cooked, add the remaining coriander and mix through.

Serves 3.

The beauty of these Stone Age soups is their simplicity. All that's required is a cohort of effusive vegetables, a short and sharp chopping session, a generous pot and a posse of ravenous gastronomes. I literally throw all the ingredients into a large pot, bring the lot to the boil, and then reduce the heat and let it simmer.

Root vegetable soup

Ingredients
4 carrots, roughly chopped
2 medium sweet potatoes, peeled and roughly chopped
2 large potatoes, peeled and roughly chopped
1 swede, peeled and roughly chopped
1 parsnip, peeled and chopped roughly
2 low salt vegetable stock cubes
1 cup coconut milk
1 very generous handful of fresh parsley, chopped roughly
1 sprig fresh rosemary
I bunch fresh coriander, chopped
6 cups water, maybe more. You will need enough to cover the top of the vegetables.

Next
Place absolutely everything in a large pot, bring to the boil and simmer, covered, for about 35 to 40 minutes until the vegetables are soft.
I like to grab a potato masher and mash the soup a little at this stage. It gives it a nice consistency and a better flavour.
Season to taste. Add a little extra coriander to each serve as a garnish.

This will serve about 6 people.

Sweet potato and pumpkin soup

This delightful concoction owes its sublime flavour to coconut milk – which was a likely Stone Age comestible.

Ingredients

1 small Kent pumpkin (or half a medium one) seeds removed and then peeled and chopped roughly
2 medium sweet potatoes, peeled and chopped roughly
1 onion, peeled and roughly chopped
2 small carrots, sliced
1 clove garlic, peeled and chopped
2 vegetable stock cubes
400 mls coconut milk
½ teaspoon of salt
Approximately 3 to 4 cups of water

NB. Not too much water or the consistency will be too runny. Too little water and it's too thick. Use your intuition.

Next

Throw the lot into a medium-sized soup pot and bring to the boil. Then simmer for about 30 minutes, or until the vegetables are soft.

Grab your blender and blend the soup until it's nice and smooth.

Garnish with finely chopped parsley.

Serves 4.

Sue's gluten-free minestrone soup

Ingredients
4 large potatoes
1 medium pumpkin (a fleshy type like Queensland
Grey is best)
1 onion
2 handfuls of broccoli
2 handfuls of cauliflower
Several handfuls of fresh peeled tomatoes. A tin of
tomatoes is fine if you have no fresh tomatoes.
2 large carrots
5 silver beet/spinach leaves
A big handful of chickpeas (2 handfuls if you love
chickpeas)
A handful of fresh green beans
2 zucchinis
2 medium-sized eggplants

Next
Peel potatoes and chop into square chunks. Peel
pumpkin and cut into chunks. Peel onion and cut
into small pieces. Place into a pot with a centimetre
(1/2 inch) of oil covering the base. Fry together for 5
minutes.
Peel and chop all the other vegetables into chunks and
add to the pot (except the chickpeas). Fry for another 4
minutes then add water to cover the vegetables.
Add the chickpeas. Add lots of tomato paste, generally
4 to 5 sachets, or one small jar. Add salt to taste. Add
basil or oregano to taste.

Leave to simmer for up to an hour.

Serves 6.

Heidi's lissome lentil soup

This gratifying concoction has a pleasing colour, a luscious texture, and a delectable taste. It goes well with sourdough bread, an old dog, and a good friend.

Ingredients
1 tablespoon olive or coconut oil
2 or 3 carrots
1 onion
I sweet potato
¾ cup red lentils
1 bay leaf
½ teaspoon cumin
½ tsp turmeric
About 1 litre vegetable stock or water with stock cube

Next

Chop onion, sweet potato and carrot and cook gently in oil on low heat for 2 or 3 minutes. Stir in turmeric and cumin and cook for further minute. Add lentils, stock or water, bay leaf and bring to the boil.

Reduce heat and simmer for 30 minutes. Remove bay leaf, puree and season to taste.

Serve with a sprinkle of fresh herbs and a dollop of sour cream or yogurt, if desired.

Serves 4.

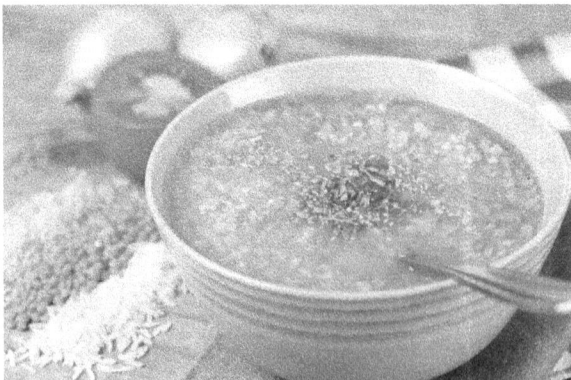

Heidi's stinging nettle soup

Stick on a pair of gardening gloves and gather some stinging nettles. Ensure you pick them from a herbicide-free area such as your own garden or neglected public land. Otherwise, a handful of healthy specimens of other edible weed varieties such as dandelions, cats' ears, purslane or chickweed can be picked and thrown into any soup, quiche or salad. Small amounts of these are best as they don't always taste that great but are very healthy. Also, younger leaves have a milder taste.
And make sure that you are correctly identifying the weed and not eating an inedible variety!
Once wilted or cooked, the plant will be safe to handle and eat and it makes a nourishing, mineral-rich brew.

Ingredients
Several large handfuls of stinging nettles
1 onion, sliced
2 large potatoes, diced
Water to cover

Next
Place onion and potatoes in a soup pot and cover with water. Bring to the boil, and simmer until the potatoes are soft.
Add your roughly chopped stinging nettles (with tougher stalks removed).
Cook for a further 5 minutes or so, then puree, and season to taste.

Serves 3.

Sue's pumpkin soup

Ingredients
One medium-sized Queensland Grey Pumpkin, peeled
and cut into rough chunks (if you can't get this then
you need an alternative, fleshy pumpkin)
4 large potatoes, peeled and chopped roughly
A little butter
1 cup organic cream
Salt and pepper to taste
Vegetable stock (either make your own or buy it)
A pot of boiling water

Next
Place the potato and pumpkin chunks into a large pot
of boiling water. When potatoes and pumpkins are soft,
drain most of the water, but leave a little at the bottom
(about an inch).
Mash the potatoes and pumpkin and add a little
butter so that it is a smooth consistency. Place the mix
back on the heat and add vegetable stock to cover the
mashed potato and pumpkin.
Pour in 1 cup of cream. Add salt and pepper to taste.
Leave to simmer for 10 minutes.

Serves 10.

Potato, leek and cauliflower soup

This sleek soup is given an interesting twist with a little fresh turmeric. If you have no fresh turmeric, consider adding a pinch of its powdered counterpart.

Ingredients
4 large potatoes, roughly chopped
1 small cauliflower, washed and broken into large florets
3 leeks, trimmed, washed and thickly sliced.
2 cloves garlic, peeled and roughly chopped
Water to cover
2 low salt vegetable stock cubes
1 teaspoon tomato paste
1 teaspoon grated fresh turmeric or ¼ teaspoon powdered turmeric (optional)
Freshly ground black pepper
Handful of parsley to garnish

Next
Grab a large soup pot and toss in everything except the fresh parsley. Make sure you pour in enough water to just cover the vegetables.
Bring to the boil, reduce heat and simmer, covered, until the vegetables are cooked. This will take about 35 minutes at the most. Stir from time to time.
When cooked, stick the lot in a blender and blast away until smooth.
Check the seasoning. It may need a little sea salt.
Garnish with fresh parsley.

Serves 4.

Apple and Plum Crisp

Preheat oven to 180 Celsius (360 Fahrenheit).

Ingredients
3 granny smith apples, peeled, cored and sliced
4 black plums, sliced. You don't need to peel them. If you can't find black plums, any type of sweet and juicy plum will do.
Juice of 2 oranges
Juice of 1 lemon

Topping
1 cup almond meal
½ cup walnuts
¼ cup desiccated coconut
1 dessertspoon honey
1 tablespoon olive oil

Next
Put sliced apples and plums in a medium size saucepan with the orange and lemon juice.
Cook over a gentle heat, covered, until the apples and plums are soft. Remove from heat and spread the fruit evenly in a baking dish.

Topping
Place the coconut, walnuts, olive oil, honey and almond meal in a food processor. Blend until everything is well-mixed. It will be quite sticky, so use a dessertspoon and place spoonfuls evenly over the fruit.

Bake in oven for about 35 minutes or until the topping is golden brown.

Serves 4.

Apple Crumble

This mostly Stone Age concoction was a favourite of all discerning dire wolves, marauding mastodons and a sturdy species of opportunistic hominids.
Preheat oven to 180 Celsius (360 Fahrenheit).

Ingredients
Fruit layer
4 large granny smith apples, peeled, cored, and sliced thickly
½ cup sultanas
Juice of one orange
Approximately 2 tablespoons water

Crumble Topping
I cup almond meal
½ cup desiccated coconut
½ cup hazelnut meal
Approximately 1 tablespoon butter
1 tablespoon honey (if this is too sweet, try 3 teaspoons or so)
½ teaspoon ground cinnamon (optional)

Next
Start with the fruit layer. Place the peeled and sliced apples into a medium saucepan with the sultanas, orange juice and water. Cook on a low heat, covered, until the apples are soft. Check frequently to ensure your apples are hydrated, but don't overdo the liquid.

When your apples are soft, remove from the heat, drain excess liquid and spread them evenly over the base of a medium-sized casserole dish.

Now make the topping
Combine the almond meal, coconut, cinnamon and

hazelnut meal in a mixing bowl. Add the butter and rub into the mix with your fingertips until it resembles coarse breadcrumbs. If it's a bit dry, add a little more butter if you want.

The next bit is a little sticky. Add the honey and do your best to mix it through. Sprinkle the topping over the apples and shove it in the oven.

Cook for about 30 minutes until the top is a sweet

Serves 4.

Mixed Berry Crumble

Ingredients
450g fresh or frozen mixed berries – a combination of
blueberries, blackberries and raspberries is nice.
Juice of one orange
¼ cup hazelnut meal
1 cup almond meal
½ cup desiccated coconut
½ teaspoon cinnamon
60g butter
1 generous tablespoon honey or maple syrup

Next
Place berries and orange juice in a saucepan and bring
to the boil. Reduce heat and simmer for about 10
minutes. Add a little water if the mixture is perilously
close to becoming a Stone Age desert. Drain excess
juice, but leave enough so the berries can still paddle,
then place them in a small-to-medium sized baking
dish.

Topping
Toss the almond meal, coconut, hazelnut meal and
cinnamon in a mixing bowl. Chop butter and rub it
into the dry mix with your fingertips until it turns into
small clumps.

Add honey or maple syrup and form into a ball.
Crumble pieces of the dough evenly over the berries.

Bake in 180 Celsius (360 Fahrenheit) oven for 25-30
minutes.

Serves 4.

Banana Sultana Orange Bliss Bake

Preheat oven to 180 Celsius (360 Fahrenheit).

Ingredients
4 ripe bananas
1 cup sultanas
Juice of two oranges
1 teaspoon vanilla essence (optional)

Next

Cut bananas in half lengthwise. Place in a lightly greased casserole dish and pour the orange juice over the top of the bananas. Toss in the sultanas and vanilla essence. Turn the bananas so they are coated all over with juice.
Place in the oven and cook for about 20 minutes. Remove from oven and turn the bananas over. Return to oven and cook for a further 20 minutes, or until bananas are soft and juicy.

Serves 4.

Coconut and Almond Bliss Balls

Ingredients
1 cup of chopped raw almonds
½ cup of sunflower kernels
 ½ cup pitted dates
A small handful of sultanas
2 tablespoons of honey

Next
Place everything in a food processor and blend until well mixed.

Roll into balls with your hands and then roll in a little more desiccated coconut. Refrigerate until firm.

Makes about 10 small balls.

WE NEED TO EAT WELL

Whole foods were the basis of Stone Age nourishment.

But now we're so far removed from this dietary existence that many of us wouldn't recognize a whole food even if it jumped on our heads and started whistling Dixie. Yet a whole food is easy to spot. It's a comestible in its natural state – intact, humble, and complete. It's as unprocessed and unrefined as possible.

Here are a few examples of whole foods:

- unpolished grains;
- beans, peas, and lentils;
- fresh fruit and vegetables; and
- unhomogenized dairy products.

A whole food has colour, vitality, micronutrients, and fibre. It's vitamin-packed, fresh, seasonal, and often locally sourced.

A whole food has a good attitude.

The body loves whole foods because it understands them. It has trouble dealing with the processed, chemically enhanced, sugar-saturated foods we eat abundantly today.

Indeed, numerous studies find a diet high in whole foods leads to:

- less cardiovascular disease;
- less cancer; and
- less Type 2 diabetes.

The recipes in this chapter all use whole foods to the core (pun intended). At heart, they're easy to make and even easier to eat.

Most of the recipes can be made in one large pot.

Just as our Stone Age ancestors would have made them.

Stone Age Secret Three
Art, Craft and Music

Art is a social determinant of our health. It doesn't cure a particular disease but benefits whatever ails you.

~ Dr John Graham-Pole, Paediatric oncologist and founder of the Arts in Medicine program.

Prehistoric people were an inventive bunch and the secret to their creativity was simplicity.

In fact, the Stone Age was a bedrock of artistic endeavour. Archaeologists have unearthed pottery, rock paintings, baskets, cooking utensils, jewellery and finely crafted bows and arrows from prehistoric camp sites, as well as flutes, horns, and drums.

It looks like our ancestors potted, painted, made crafts and played music with simple tools and natural materials.

It's good for our physical and mental health to get creative, especially when we use basic equipment and natural products to produce things of beauty and utility.

POTTERY

It's unlikely Stone Age people potted for leisure, but pottery today is very much a recreational pursuit as well as a powerful form of self-expression. The hands, especially, love to be used and it's no wonder – they're the most complex and sensitive of any mammal.

Pottery is excellent for our mental health. Here's why:

- It's calming and soothing. Clay is sleek, cool and pliable when wet. It feels good to shape and handle and its suppleness and velvety texture encourages us to soften inwardly;

- It's satisfying to shape clay into something useful and beautiful;

- It's meditative. It's hard to feel tense when we're shaping clay. Our breath slows down. Our bodies slow down. Our thoughts diminish. Clay-shaping stills and quiets the mind;

- It alleviates pain. When our minds focus on something engaging, we're less likely to notice our physical ailments. Pottery is also pleasurable and floods us with natural painkillers;

- It encourages attention to detail. Decorating our creations requires that we reproduce a design from head to paper to object in such a way as to look attractive;

- It builds concentration. We must watch what we're doing or the clay will collapse;

- It's great for arthritis. Shaping clay increases blood flow to the hand and finger joints and stretches the muscles of the fingers and palms. Clay work brings warmth and energy to the hands which, in turn, reduces pain and inflammation;

- It's sensual. Our fingers have a high concentration of touch receptors and a large part of the brain handles sensory input from our hands; and

- It's therapeutic for depression, anxiety and bipolar disorder because getting together with others lessens feelings of isolation and sadness.

PAINTING

Prehistoric cave painters used earthy colours – orange,

yellow, and red-brown – which they made by crushing minerals and binding them together with egg and animal fat. They painted animals, hunting expeditions and strange half-human, half-beast hybrids that author Graham Hancock speculates were created while they were high on plant psychedelics.

Painting, like pottery, focuses and concentrates the mind. It also teaches colour, perspective and design. Painting provides an emotional outlet and joining a group class is an enlivening social activity.
Here are two Stone Age painting styles you may like to try:

Watercolour. A truly ancient medium, watercolour was used to illuminate ancient Egyptian manuscripts and for hundreds of years it's been the preferred style of botanical artists and science illustrators. To this day, watercolour painting features prominently in wildlife illustrations and naturalist field guides (Wikipedia).

Tempera. Quintessentially prehistoric, tempera paintings are found on early Egyptian sarcophagi and Western paintings from the first century AD. It's also called 'egg tempera' and made of coloured pigment mixed with water-soluble binders such as egg yolk. It dries fast and lasts for millennia.

MUSIC

Stone Age people made music with flutes, drums, and horns. Excavations at Hohle Fels cave near the city of Ulm, Germany, dug up three flutes – two made from mammoth ivory and one from the wing bone of a vulture. In 1986, bone flutes were found in China dating back to 6,000 BCE. They each have five to eight holes and are made from bird bone. One of the flutes is still playable. It's also speculated that pieces of flint found in various European caves were used for cave-entrance wind chimes.

Even before human-made instruments, people made music by clapping hands, hitting stones together and, of course, with their voices.

Music-making is excellent for mental health because it:

- improves memory, motor skills and auditory processing abilities;
- refines people skills. Musicians become attuned to the rhythms and tones of music and they can transfer this skill to human relationships. This means they become adept at discerning subtle changes in other people's moods and behaviour and they can adjust themselves to deal sensitively with most interpersonal interactions;
- develops empathy because of this ability to tune in to another's feelings and moods;
- increases ear sensitivity;
- improves patience. Learning an instrument requires persistence and consistent practise. Overcoming our tendency to give up and criticise ourselves means we must cultivate equanimity;
- encourages self-discipline. To improve our playing we need to practise. And practise requires setting aside time each day to work with our instrument; and
- satisfies the brain's love of challenge and novelty. Learning a new piece of music gives the brain something complex and interesting to do. It also builds a healthier brain by increasing the connections between neurons.

DRUMMING

The primitive drumming circle is emerging as a significant therapeutic tool in the modern technological age.

~ Michael Drake

Drums are one of our most ancient and pervasive instruments and we're not the only species that drums. Animals do, too. Non-human percussionists include macaques, gorillas and chimpanzees. There's even a drumming rodent known as the kangaroo rat.

Group drumming is especially good. It primes the body to release endorphins and natural opiates. It also reduces anxiety because it lowers blood pressure and encourages deep relaxation. Dr Barry Bittman is a neurologist. He's a passionate advocate of music as a stress reducer and he created a drum playing music therapy called Health Rhythms. It improves mood while exercising brain cells and their synaptic connections.

'Group drumming,' says Dr Bittman, 'tunes our biology, orchestrates our immunity, and enables healing to begin.' It may even assist cancer treatment. He found that group drumming increases the number of cancer-killing cells, which boosts the immune system.
It also helps us to reconnect with each other. We feel more of a sense of belonging because group drumming decreases feelings of isolation and helps us be with others at a deeper level.

Drumming also activates the whole brain. Drum rhythms somehow synchronise both brain hemispheres, harmonising the brain and leading to new and creative insights and ideas. It's a pathway to altered states of consciousness. Even short drumming sessions can double alpha brain wave activity. According to Barry Quinn, PhD, the brain changes from beta waves, which are prevalent when we're busy, to alpha waves which calm and relax us. This leads to a sense of joy and wellbeing.

Hand drums are a great instrument for novice musicians. They're portable, easy to tune, and can be used in a variety of musical styles and settings. Here are five hand drums to consider:

Djembe – a rope-tuned, skin-covered drum played with bare hands. It is very loud. It is one of the most versatile drums because it produces a wide variety of sounds. It heralds from West Africa and is traditionally played by men. Weighs between 5 and 13kg (11–29 lbs) so it can get quite heavy.

Bongo – This two-sized drum is thought to have originated in the eastern region of Cuba, but it's likely to have African origins. The larger drum in Spanish is called the hembra (female) and the smaller drum is called the macho (male). Its pitch is higher than most other hand drums.

Conga – A tall, narrow, single-headed Cuban drum. It stands 75cm tall (30in) and is usually played in sets of two to four with the fingers and palms of the hand. It's commonly heard in Latin music such as reggae and salsa, but it's in many other popular music styles too.

Doumbek – or Goblet drum. Used mostly in the

Middle East, Northern Africa and Eastern Europe. Played under the arm or resting on the leg. The touch is light and uses lots of quick rolls and rhythms initiated by the fingers.

Cajon – Fun and versatile and very simple to play. It's a box drum large enough to sit on. It's played with the palms, fists and fingers and possibly originated in coastal Peru.

SINGING

The human voice was probably the first musical instrument. Our ancestors likely began with humming, whistling, yelling, clicking, yawning and coughing. Loud, rhythmic group singing was probably used while making food, during rituals and preparing for battle. Raised voices also intimidate predators and opponents.

It's also thought that early hominids used soft, relaxing humming to maintain group contact and to warn each other of danger.

Benefits of singing

Singing is therapeutic emotionally and physically. It exercises and develops the lungs. It's also energising, good for posture, and lifts mood. Join a choir. It gets you out of the house and takes your mind off your troubles.

It's a timeless pleasure. And because it's pleasurable, it releases endorphins, the body's feel-good chemicals. This bolsters the immune system and enlivens the mind, body and spirit. Oxytocin levels – remember that amazing hormone I talked about in Chapter One? – also increase and this boosts the immune system also.

Creating your own music with simple instruments is wonderfully satisfying. And it's easy. Put aside 10 minutes a day and aim for regular, consistent practise.

Other Stone Age instruments

Here are three more Stone Age instruments for you to consider.

Flute – Light, sweet-sounding and portable, it provides a perfect Stone Age musical interlude in today's frantic world.

Horns – The smaller the better.

Recorder – Simple, light and portable, with a humble tone to add atmosphere to any gathering.

DANCING

Dancing is an ancient form of self-expression and paintings of dancing Stone Age people are found on prehistoric Spanish rock wall paintings.

Any type of dancing is good. It's great exercise, gets you out of the house and is a fabulous way to meet people. Here are some of its many mental and physical benefits:

Enhanced flexibility: Dancing requires bending and stretching and this warms and extends muscles and takes them through their full range of movement.

Increased strength: Dancing forces our muscles to resist our body's pull. This active resistance builds muscle and bone.

Wellbeing: Any physical activity increases calm by releasing endorphins and decreases stress by lowering our blood pressure and taking our mind off problems. Dancing is also a social activity and a good social life reduces anxiety and increases confidence.

Endurance: Dance is strong physical exercise and most physical exercise increases our ability to withstand physical and mental hardship.

Balance: We feel better when our lives are in balance. Dancing helps harmonise our mind and body as we feel our way through the dance steps. On a physical level, dancing strengthens the small muscles of our ankles and the large muscles of the calves and thighs. On a mental level, as our balance improves, we're able to stand on our own two feet with poise and confidence. We feel stronger and more independent.

Bellydancing

Bellydancing is quintessentially Stone Age.
It combines all the benefits of dancing with the health-promoting features of earthing because it's done with bare feet. Its fluid movements increase circulation, tone all the major muscle groups and produce a more graceful and supple body. It's a meditative, grounding dance and many practitioners report feeling stronger and more supported by the earth. Bellydancing's also great for people who slouch because it lifts the shoulders.

WE NEED TO FOSTER CREATIVITY

Stone Age people were an artistic bunch and they invented a wealth of pursuits for us to try including painting, playing an instrument, singing, pottery and dancing.

Whatever art, craft, or musical instrument we take up, we can be sure it will improve our wellbeing. This is because it's good for our physical and mental health to get creative.

Creative pastimes increase our patience, self-discipline, concentration and attention to detail. They can also be meditative, calming and soothing, as well as providing us with an emotional and social outlet.

The brain also thrives on challenge and novelty and art, craft, and music are ideal because there's always something new to learn – a new piece of music, a new painting technique, a new way of stitching a quilt.

And it's never too late to learn. I took up piano at 43 and although I'm very much an amateur, I can now play dozens of simple jazz and blues pieces.

Stone Age Secret Four Retreats

Your own space, man, it's so important. That's why we were doomed because we didn't have any. It is like monkeys in a zoo. They die. You know, everything needs to be left alone.

~ George Harrison, *I, Me, Mine*

ENOUGH ALREADY

It was Day Three and I'd had enough. I'd had enough of the gong that perforated my eardrums and woke me from slumber every morning at 4am. I'd had enough of the silence and the chanting and the 40 other captives I neither knew nor cared about. I'd had enough of the meditation and the guru's videotaped talks which ended with yet another round of tendon-shriveling chants.

My legs ached, my back buckled under and my spine had collapsed with the grace of a swooning bull elephant. And in an eerie sub-plot, I developed an antipathy to my meditation cushion bordering on the demonic. I'd landed in Dante's Eighth Circle of Hell. And there were still seven days to go.

I told a retreat facilitator I could no longer cope. I told her about my legs and back and spine. My voice was whiny, like a peevish toddler's. And the nice lady told me to go back to my room and do yoga. I didn't have the strength to argue. This was fortunate because her advice got me through the next week with limbs intact, spine elevated and sanity partly restored.

That was eight years ago. This is what I know now: I endured this 10 day retreat like a sulky child but it was exactly what I needed and my life improved from that point onwards.

A SIMPLE LIFE

Life was hard in the Stone Age but it was simple. People's jobs were clear-cut. No one was pummeled with choice, swamped by celebrities or rendered comatose in front of the television. The internet, smart phones, Twitter, Instagram and Facebook were thousands of years away.

Today, everything is noisy and fast and demands attention. It's hard to stay mindful and to separate the trivial from the essential in this chaos. Even supermarket shopping is enough to enfeeble the body and deflate the spirit.

We live in a world unrecognizable to our Stone Age ancestors. Is it any wonder we're stressed?

But there is a way back.

A retreat is usually thought of as a strategic manoeuvre undertaken to avoid an imminent threat. So the concept of a retreat suggests failure to withstand attack, surrender in the face of superior opposition, or the incapacity to confront a destructive force.

But retreat can also be an opportunity and sometimes we must remove ourselves from the distractions and disturbances of modern life to regain perspective and clarity.

A personal perspective from Suellen H.

'For me, the need to retreat grew more urgent gradually. Repressive coping became the norm. No major trauma. No catastrophic event. No great upheaval. But each day became an ordeal, an endurance test that left me exhausted and defeated. I have no idea why. I just knew that I had to find a way to change the pattern. It clashed starkly and contorted the shape of my days. It had to go.

In the end I went – went away to a retreat that helped me cut through the impenetrable thicket of strangler vines that had slowly snaked their way around my life, squeezing out all energy and interest. Retreating helped me to gain a different perspective and to see that the oppressive jungle grew from my own imaginings.

Stepping back, I could see how to recognise the growth of unhelpful preoccupations and learn how to restrain them, retrain them. And best of all, retreating helped me to discover paths to a more peaceful, healthy and rewarding way of being. These paths too will require constant maintenance to keep them navigable. At least now I welcome the work.'

BENEFITS OF A RETREAT

In my experience, retreats provide sanctuary from the busy world and give me space and time to do my inner work. I also get to quiet my mind and rest my body which brings hidden gifts and possibilities to the fore. What's more, I'm served healthy food by happy people in a meditative and peaceful environment. Retreats invite me to look at the world with fresh eyes. They bring me home to myself.

Retreats also:

- encourage new ideas and fresh ways of being in the world;
- foster clarity of mind;
- give insight into the mind and how it works, especially its need for control and projection and its habitual urge to live in the past (through memory) and the future (through imagination); and
- offer us challenging tasks to expand our tolerance for mental and physical discomfort.

Most of all, retreats give us the best of the Stone Age without the predators, extremes of temperature, disease or starvation.

Best of Stone Age	Retreats
Plenty of peace and quiet	Plenty of peace and quiet
No gadgets	No gadgets (usually)
No telemarketers	No telemarketers
Healthy, organic food	Healthy, organic food
Surrounded by nature	Surrounded by nature (usually)
No celebrities	Maybe a few if they're on retreat themselves, but they'll be keeping a low profile. In any case, most of them will be at the insanely expensive re-treats for zillionaires that I write about further on.
No advertising	No advertising
Slower pace of life	Slower pace of life
No supermarkets	No supermarkets

WHEN IS IT TIME TO RETREAT?

Most of us rush through life at light speed and it's hard to know when to stop.

It's time to retreat if:

You're exhausted.

You hate your job more than usual.

Your family is driving you nuts.

You're driving yourself nuts.

You're driving everyone else nuts.

Your dog ignores you.

And you definitely need to retreat if:

You sense something missing in your life and you don't know what.

You feel your life lacks direction, purpose and meaning.

You're in a rut.

Your spouse has left you.

You've left your spouse.

Where to go

Retreats are held at ashrams, monasteries, yoga studios, private houses and purpose-built centres. Some retreats are more physically challenging – for example, those conducted in the desert or forest with minimal shelter and basic facilities.

Who's in charge?

Retreats are run by spiritual teachers, yogis, vision quest guides, monks, counsellors, psychologists, nutritionists, cancer survivors and therapists of all kinds.

I'd suggest you do some research on the retreat facilitator before you go. Google their name, inquire about their organization or spiritual tradition (if they have one), and read books or articles they've written. You'll quickly discern whether this person needs further investigation before committing yourself to spending time with them.

Retreat length

Retreats vary in length from half a day to 10 days. Some last several years.

Extreme retreat interlude (including the Cave Lion award for retreat of the epoch)

And the nominations are:

Jesus of Nazareth: This spirited luminary spent 40 days and 40 nights wandering the desert. He emerged feverish and half-starved after being stalked by the Prince of Darkness who taunted him mercilessly, told him to turn stones into bread and finally dared him to jump off a temple.

Gautama Buddha: It's been over 2,000 years since this amiable sage sat under a Bodhi tree for 49 days. It was worth the wait because he figured out no less than Four Noble Truths:

- The truth of suffering (dukkha).
- The truth of the cause of suffering (samudaya).
- The truth of the end of suffering (nirhodha).
- The truth of the path that frees us from suffering (magga).

The Sanctuary: This place is a rehab/retreat for the brain-numbingly rich in Byron Bay, Australia. I've included it in extreme retreats because it costs an extreme fortune. Clients stay in a Balinese-style villa on the beach. At the time of writing (August, 2013) it costs about $34,000 for a week's stay and $135,000 for four weeks. People have a personal chef, a live-in carer, therapists of all modalities and a soap menu. Yes, you read that right: a soap menu.

The Great Retreat: Extends a mind-boggling three years, three months and three days during which its participants are expected to maintain complete silence. In the winter of 2010, a small group of people went into a 500 acre valley in the foothills of the Chiricahua mountains in Southern Arizona. They hope to emerge transformed.

And the winner of the Cave Bear award for Retreat of the Epoch is: Dianne Perry.

Cave in the Snow: Diane Perry (aka Tenzin Palmo) is a British woman who spent 12 years on retreat in a cave 13,000 feet high on a Himalayan mountain. It was as Stone Age as it gets – freezing cold, wild animals, floods, snow, and rock falls. She grew her own food and slept in a traditional wooden meditation box in which she could not lay down. And she was snow bound for eight months of the year.

WHAT TO EXPECT ON RETREAT

Retreats may involve a combination of meditation, fasting, chanting, bodywork, relaxation, self-inquiry, journal keeping and discussion. The food is healthy, the surroundings quiet and the distractions minimal. Mobile phones, iPads, laptops and other electronic appendages are discouraged, as are drinking, smoking and hallucinogens – both human-made and naturally occurring.

Although there are exceptions. Like Ayahuasca, for example.

Ayahuascan intermission

Deep in the Amazon jungle, shamans invite retreat participants to drink Ayahuasca – a sacred plant medicine also known as the Vine of the Soul. It's a bitter tea made from two Amazonian plants, one of which contains the powerful hallucinogen DMT (Dimethyltryptamine). DMT occurs in trace amounts in mammals, including humans, and when taken orally it induces a heightened state of consciousness. Westerners in search of meaning are racing to Ayahuasca ceremonies where they hope to experience powerful visions and life-changing epiphanies. There's a wonderful DVD by Richard Meech called *The Vine of the Soul: Encounters with Ayahuasca* and it captures the visionary experience from a naturopath's and an accountant's viewpoint (also available as a PDF download – see Resources).

Other types of retreat

Some retreats are tightly structured with intense meditation sessions from pre-dawn to early evening. Others retreats are less demanding. For example, a macrobiotic knitting retreat in Scotland involves nothing more than knitting as much as you like and showing up for meals and an after dinner chat around a roaring fire.

THINGS TO CONSIDER BEFORE BOOKING A RETREAT

How much time do you have? A day? A week? A month?

How much money do you have? If you're inclined to stinginess, remember this: It's your health. And besides, how much do you spend on clothes, gadgets and entertainment each year?

Do you have any meditation experience? Many retreats require extensive meditation periods.

If you choose a meditation-intensive retreat, find out how much meditation is involved. If you're new to meditation, long hours of sitting are painful and you'll need to practice beforehand.

I considered myself an experienced meditator when I attended the 10-day Vipassana Buddhist retreat I mention at the start of this chapter, but I was ill-prepared for the hours of sitting. My advice is to work up to at least 45 minutes of meditation per day for at least a month prior to your retreat.

How much discomfort can you stand? Some retreats are five star; others would scare a Spartan warrior. You might be best to start middle-of-the-road. This likely means a two-to-three day retreat.

How far do you want to travel? Local? Interstate? Overseas?
What food are you prepared to ingest? Remember, it's about challenging old habits, so don't let unusual or unfamiliar food be the deciding factor.

How to prepare

Retreats are challenging. You're in an unusual environment with unfamiliar people. This is good. That's the
idea. Challenge reveals new possibilities and hidden
strengths. But it helps to prepare.

Physical preparation

Start a daily 20-minute stretch routine, especially if
you're going on a retreat that requires extended meditation periods. Sitting still is easier if you've got flexibility
and stamina. Also, a physical practice of any kind is
grounding and will help if you feel lost or anxious. The
best book I know is *Stretching* by Bob Anderson and
Jean Anderson (see Resources).
If you're already a meditator, good. If not, start now.
Begin several weeks before you leave home. Start with
five minutes. Sit comfortably, with your spine erect and
focus on your breath. Then build up to 10, 15, 20, and
then 30 to 45 minutes. Grab yourself a book on meditation.

A five-minute meditation redux

Sit comfortably on the floor or a chair. Ensure your
spine is erect. Rest your hands on your thighs with
your palms facing up or down. Close your eyes and
bring your attention inward. Focus on the space behind
your closed eyelids. Soften your face. Tuck your chin
in gently. Let your shoulders fall away from your ears.
Breathe gently and evenly. Notice your inhale and
exhale. Sit still, be silent, and disregard any thoughts
that arise. Simply let them float by without your
interest.

Food

Most retreats serve vegetarian food. If this is unappealing, go gradually meatless in the weeks prior to the retreat. You could even try a few of the recipes in my Wholefoods chapter.

Reduce or eliminate tea and coffee. Most retreat organizers will advise you to reduce and then stop your caffeine intake a few days before the retreat. This is good advice. I'm a recalcitrant creature, however, and way too fond of tea so I ignore this advice. This means I get a horrible headache. Solution – I take two aspirin to the retreat with me. I figure this humble medicament fails to contravene the aforementioned hallucinogenic ban, but, strictly speaking, it's still a drug. I'm human.

I console myself with this story: I once went on a five-day retreat with 20 others. We were required to juice-fast for three of those days. I hate juice-fasts but did as I was told. At retreat's end, I discovered half the participants had smuggled in enough food to feed a small island nation. So while I was internally fermenting and feeling tetchier and more deprived by the nanosecond, those treacherous fiends were gorging on lamingtons and crackers and luxury cheeses.

The mind, other people and how to cope with them

Your mind loves to be boss and it fights to keep it that way. It will distract you with sad stories and embarrassing memories. It will exhume past hurts, jealousies, fears and disappointments. It will highlight anything and everything that annoys you about everyone and everything on the retreat. If that fails to work, it will run an even tackier mental movie with you as hero or victim and all designed to pull you back into your personal drama.

To overcome this you must actively ignore the mind.

But how?

John Paul Sartre said, 'Hell is other people'.

For most of us that's true, unless we recognize the ego in ourselves and others. To prepare to be with strangers for extended periods, get hold of Eckhart Tolle's *A New Earth*. Read the entire book and then go back and re-read the chapters on the structure and content of the ego. It's by far the best explication of what the human ego is, how it originated and how it's maintained. This book is practical, useful and wise. It will help you deal with the incessant mental commentary your mind spins about your fellow retreaters.

How to prepare for silence

Many retreats have periods of what's called Noble Silence where people neither speak to nor acknowledge each other. It can be strange and uncomfortable to be with people and to say nothing because we're conditioned to fill silence with talk. But be brave. Before long it's a beautiful and expansive thing to be with other humans and to feel little need to be interesting or entertaining. In my experience I got to relate to people on a deeper and more positive level. You will need to prepare for quiet. Experiment with living in silence for longer and longer times in the weeks before a retreat. Resist the urge to play music in your car and home, even if it's only for a short while.

See if you can allow more silence in your interactions with family and friends. Even if means you wait an extra second or two before responding. Again, spiritual teacher Eckhart Tolle is helpful here. His book *Stillness Speaks* is a wonderful preparation for silence and I'd advise anyone serious about retreating to read it.

And speaking of serious, here's my favourite retreat joke:
A young man hopes to forge a career as a monk but first he must demonstrate his dedication by spending a year in retreat at his local monastery. Speaking is forbidden except for once a month when the abbot meets with his prospective students. Even then, only two words are permitted.

At the end of the first month, the abbot calls the young man to his side.

'How is everything?'

'More food,' says the aspiring monk.

The abbot nods wisely and dismisses him.

A month passes and the abbot once again summons the young man to his side.

'How is everything?'

'More blankets,' says the young man.
The abbot nods and sends him away.

At the end of the third month, the abbot summons the aspiring monk to his side.

'How is everything?'

'More books,' says the young man.

The abbot smiles sagely and dismisses him.

At the end of the fourth month, the aspirant once again stands before the abbot.

'How is everything?'

'I quit,' says the young man, throwing his prayer beads, yoga mat and dried goji berries out the window before storming from the room.

The abbot's assistant enters to check on the commotion.

'Is everything all right, your Holiness?'

'Indeed it is Grasshopper. I'm delighted the young rascal's gone. He's done nothing but complain since he got here.'

WE NEED RETREATS

Retreats remove us from the busy world and give us space and time to do our inner work. Retreats help quieten the mind and rest the body and invite us to view the world with less cynical eyes.
Most of all, retreats give us the best of the Stone Age without the predators, extremes of temperature, disease or starvation.

Retreats bring us home to ourselves.

Stone Age Secret Five
Community

The village is coming back, like it or not.
~ David Brin, *Tomorrow Happens*

COMMUNITY

When I think of community I envision connection and support and general social cohesion. I bet Stone Age people lived and breathed community in much the same way they lived and breathed nature. And I also bet they'd have no idea what we're talking about when we say we've lost a sense of community because community for them must have been like the sky and the rain and the trees. Simply there.

But all is not lost. Here are two innovative ways community is reasserting itself in the modern world.

GIFT CIRCLES

It's not Christmas, so why am I sitting in a circle with eight people as we shower each other with gifts?
It's because I belong to a gift circle, which I've heard is a modern adaption of an ancient practice.

Whether it really is ancient I have no idea. But who cares because in my experience it's a fine and noble way to build relationships and restore a semblance of community in our fragmented society.

I love gift circles because they build an alternative economy based on sharing where people give of their possessions, talents and time with no expectation of return.

I got the idea to start my own circle after reading the book Sacred Economics by writer and self-described "de-growth activist" Charles Eisenstein. He believes we need to encourage more compassionate and trusting relationships and the key to this is to become givers rather than consumers.

Sacred Economics offers creative ways to reduce our dependence on the money economy, which in turn helps rebuild community and restore our connection to the natural world.

Gift circles are a perfect way to build community because our needs are met by each other rather than by corporations and shopping centres. This means we spend less money and waste fewer resources. For example, in my gift circle olive oil tins, glass jars and polystyrene boxes are re-used for gardening and storage projects.

The beauty of it all is that we share our surplus and this inspires generosity, trust and goodwill. It also discourages hoarding and keeps our wealth moving. I once thought the adage "Those who ask shall receive" was really corny. I no longer think it's corny because I've seen it in action.

But before we receive, it's nice to give first.

How a gift circle works

You need between ten and twenty people. It's important everyone is clear from the start that it's not a bartering system, although people are welcome to barter on the side. The key idea is that people share their goods and services as a gift without expectation of anything in return.

A gift circle comprises three rounds.

Round One: Everyone sits in a circle and takes
turns expressing one or two needs they have. For
example, a lift to the airport, a ladder, a bag of lemons,
a massage, someone to walk their dog, etc.
As each person expresses a need, others in the circle
can interject with suggestions and offers on how to
meet the need. When everyone's had their turn, it's time
for round two.

Round Two: We go around the circle again. This time,
each person offers an item, or a service or an idea
or suggestion that he or she would like to give. For
example, babysitting, baking, how to solve a particular
problem, clothes, or the use of something such as a
wheelbarrow or a chainsaw. Again, as each person
shares, anyone can speak up and say, "I'd like that," or "I
know someone who could use one of those."

As each round unfurls, a scribe records everything and
sends an email to group members that evening or the
next day. This way it's easy to remember everyone's
needs and offerings and what's been received.

Also, it's essential that offers are followed-up or the gift
circle will breed resentment and cynicism rather than
community. Therefore, someone in the group must take
on the role of follow-upper and be prepared to keep it
all together. Consider it as a service to the world.

Actually, it's not very hard to keep it all together. I don't
think I've had to follow up anything. People naturally
and easily commit to their offers – it seems to be the
way a gift circle operates. But initially at least, it needs
to be watched and nurtured until there comes a point
when it flows seamlessly.

Round Three: This round is where each person takes it in turn to thank others in the group, or they may thank the group as a whole. For example, I might thank a member of the group for the bag of lemons they gave me last circle. Someone else might thank another member for a suggestion they made which helped solve a problem.

Whatever the nature of the thanks, this round is very important because in community, the witnessing of others' generosity inspires generosity in those who witness it. It also confirms this group is giving to each other, that gifts are recognised and acknowledged and that my own gifts will be recognised and appreciated as well.

Although a gift circle is easy to start, it's a challenge to keep it alive. This is because people are busy and also because alternative economies still face huge resistance from the money economy juggernaut.

Indeed, it takes time, energy and commitment from all members to build a structure strong enough to withstand the cult of productivity and money's hypnotic allure.

Other impediments to maintaining a circle include our anxiety about appearing selfish or acquisitive when expressing needs and our discomfort about receiving gifts when there's no expectation of reciprocation. I no longer think these impediments are serious because what I can say from my gift circle experience is, yes, there is anxiety and discomfort at first and it soon passes.

Admittedly, there were moments our circle struggled, especially during the winter months and numbers dropped. I fretted that it was all falling in a heap and we'd be lured back to consumerism. Instead, we're still here, giving and receiving with increasing trust and confidence.

Gift circles, wonderful as they are, still struggle in a money-centred culture and yet they're more essential than ever. They foster community, encourage generosity and help us all live more simply and thoughtfully.

THE DATTI: MONEY IN REVERSE

Civilisation's most fatal folly was monetization and propertizing of the natural world that is humanity's great commons.

- Joe Bageant, Nine Billion Little Feet.

Recently, I spent a day in a friend's shed where we made 32 dattis over a Bunsen burner. The datti is a beautiful pewter coin that might look and feel like money but it has a very different agenda.

Jesse Dow, from Boulder, Colorado is its creator. Here's how he chose its name:

"Datti is one of about 20 Sanskrit words for 'gift'. Have you ever heard the story about the Inuit and how they have 20 words for snow? It's said that they see snow in a profoundly intimate and complex way compared to the rest of us because they have created an intimate and complex language structure and vocabulary around it. There's the heavy snow of spring, and then there's a light deep powder, and also the icy snow that's good for making igloos -- and only they know what the 17 others are.

I was researching words for gift in various 'dead' languages because I wanted the name of the coin to be something that didn't really belong to anyone, or to any specific present-day culture.

When I looked up Sanskrit, I was completely blown away by how many words they had for gift -- like the Inuit's twenty words for snow. I can't even imagine what it must have been like to live in a culture with such a language. Imagine being able to easily distinguish between 20 different forms of gifts.

Anyway, I fell upon 'datti' because it's what my youngest son called me for the first four years or so of his life. I don't know if he was unable to pronounce the word 'daddy' or if he just liked 'datti' better, but that's what he called me. I saw the word and immediately fell in love. Which is really the point, right?
And so even the name might also reflect a time when we have recovered, and even deepened, the ancient mastery of giving and receiving gifts. Imagine that world!"

So what exactly is a datti?

A datti is a form of money that flows in the reverse direction from all other money that has ever existed. Although a datti coin might look and feel like money, its purpose is to mark the gift economy's ethos with a visible, attractive and concrete symbol. In a nutshell, it travels with a gift and is not used as an exchange for a product or service.

Since the ascent of agriculture, a trade-based economy
has dominated and its currency (money) flows in the
opposite direction to everything else in the world. This
is because money serves as a tool of exchange.
This leads to the situation where everything that can
be monetized and commodified flows in one direction,
while money, which is being exchanged for these goods
or services, flows in the other.

So what we end up with is this: Earth's resources flow
one way while money flows in the other. With a datti
currency, however, Earth's bounty and the datti flow in
the same direction.

For example: I want to give you a gift such as a bunch
of roses. When I give you this gift, I also include a
datti. This marks the giving of the gift and prompts you
to think about a gift you can make to someone else.
When you're ready to give a gift, you do so and with it
you pass the datti to the receiver of your gift. This then
prompts them to think about someone to whom they
can gift something. And so it goes until one day we all
wake up in a world of gifts.

It took me a while to get this because I'm conditioned
to operate within the trade-based economy's
fundamental precept: fair trade. And so is just about
everyone else.

This means most of us want something as cheaply as
possible, so we negotiate for a better deal. And the
people with whom we are dealing are also trying to
get a better deal out of us. Furthermore, trade based
transactions are always initiated by the buyer who, as
we've seen, is usually furthering his or her needs rather

than the needs of the other.

But the datti, as you've probably guessed by now, represents a complete reversal of this mindset because, ultimately, it rewards giving, not accumulating.

Anyone can make this little beauty and all you need is a sense of adventure and a coin-making mold. You can read all about the datti and how it works via thedatti. org.

We Need Community

As Jane Addams, the early 20th century social and political activist, said, "The good we secure for ourselves is precarious and uncertain until it is secured for all of us and incorporated into our common life."

Community is worth building because it secures the good for all of us. It promotes social cohesion and trust and keeps us connected through a web of mutual co-operation. We look out for each other in community. We form bonds and strengthen friendships.

Community also lessens the need for money and helps us reduce waste and live more compatibly with the earth, our only home.

EPILOGUE

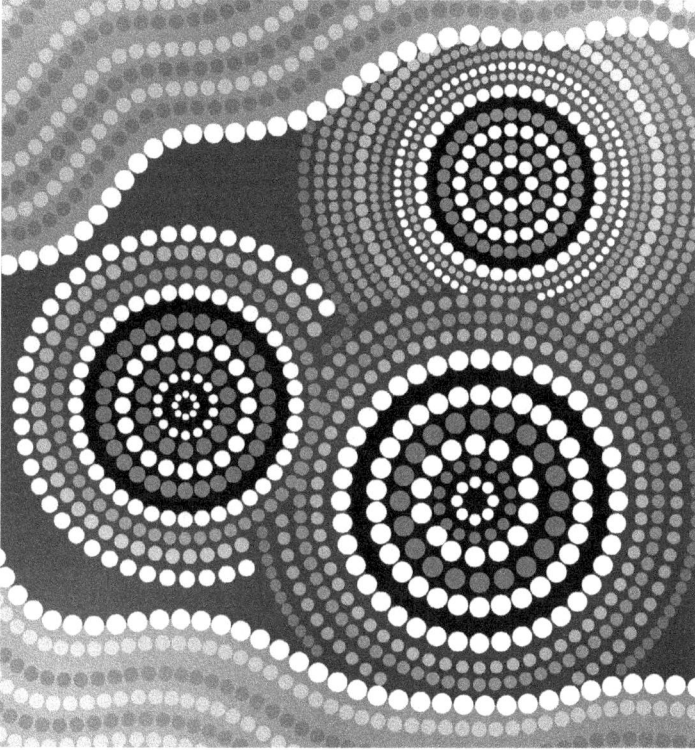

I'm glad I never lived in the Stone Age. It was harsh and dangerous.

Nevertheless, it holds the key to a saner life in a mad world.

The Stone Age was quieter, less polluted, and more communal. People were outside often, got plenty of exercise, and ate food the human body recognizes and understands. Everyone had their place and jobs were clear-cut and essential for group survival. Consumerism did not rule the world. Humans were spared the depredations of telemarketers, advertising, and traffic jams.

Our lives may be sleeker, more technologically dazzling and materially comfortable than ever before, yet we've lost something. We've lost our connection with nature and with what keeps our bodies strong and our minds robust.

The five Stone Age secrets to a healthier life are the very things our ancestors took for granted: nature; wholefoods; art, craft, and music; retreat and community.

These days, despite our prosperity we are more fragile than ever. Millions of people are lonely, undernourished, depressed, chronically ill, spiritually hungry and drug addled.

This book can help free you from what writer Maria Popova calls the 'cult of productivity' that keeps us chasing material comfort and economic growth at the expense of inner contentment and physical wellbeing.

RESOURCES AND REFERENCES

Introduction

Goscienski, Philip J. 2006, 'Stone Agers were not so short-lived', *Stone Age Doc*, stoneagedoc.com/Short_lived_Stone_Age.htm

Levine, Bruce E. 2013, 'Living in America will drive you insane – literally', *Salon*, 1 August, salon.com/2013/07/31/living_in_america_will_drive_you_insane_literally_partner/

Short, Michael 2013, 'Easing troubled minds', *The Age*, 20 August.

Wood, Stephanie 2013, 'All the lonely people', *The Sydney Morning Herald*, 5 September, smh.com.au/lifestyle/life/all-the-lonely-people-20130826-2skkz.html

Chapter One: Nature

American Heart Association, startwalkingnow.org

Doidge, Norman 2007, *The Brain that Changes Itself,* Scribe Publications, Melbourne, ch. 3, p. 91.

Meech, Richard (film director) 2010, Vine of the Soul: *Encounters with Ayahuasca,* Meech Grant Productions Ltd. Available to purchase as a DVD or a downloadable PDF file from vineofthesoul.myshopify.com

Ober, C., Sinatra, S. T. MD & Zucker, M. 2010, *Earthing,* Ober, C., Sinatra, S. T. M.D. & Zucker, M., Basic Health Publications Inc., Laguna Beach, California.

Rodale News 2011, '8 astonishing benefits of walking', *Mother Nature Network*, 11 November, mnn.com/ health/fitness-well-being/stories/8-astonishing-benefits-of-walking

Tolle, Eckhart 2003, *Stillness Speaks*, Hodder Headline Australia, Sydney.

'What is Nordic Walking?', *WiseGEEK*, http:// www.wisegeek.net/what-is-nordic-walking. htm#didyouknowout

Chapter Two: Whole foods

Bittman, Mark 2007, *How to Cook Everything Vegetarian,* 2nd edn, Houghton Mifflin Harcourt, Hoboken, NJ/United States.

Jensen, Tanya Lousdal 2013, 'Stone Age hunters liked their carbs', *ScienceNordic,* 4 January, sciencenordic. com/stone-age-hunters-liked-their-carbs

Parker-Pope, Tara 2013, 'Is organic better? Ask a fruit fly', *The New York Times,* 17 April, http://well.blogs. nytimes.com/2013/04/17/is-organic-better-ask-a-fruit-fly/?_r=0

Thomas, Anna 1996, *The New Vegetarian Epicure*, Knopf Publications, New York.

Chapter Three: Art, Craft and Music

Desy, Phylameana Lila, 'Therapeutic drumming', *About. com Holistic Healing,* healing.about.com/od/drums/tp/ drum-therapy.htm

Wikipedia.org/painting

About.com Drum Therapy. Lots of information about the therapeutic effects of drumming.

Types of drums:
Moresingingplease.com

Pugh, Merridy 2013, '*The art of picnicking*', midlifexpress.com, 8 May, midlifexpress.com/art-picknicking/

Sethi, Meera Lee 2009, 'Does art heal?' *Greater Good: The Science of a Meaningful Life,* University of California, Berkeley, http://greatergood.berkeley.edu/article/item/does_art_heal

'Stone Age DIY: How Neolithic man decorated his house with homemade paint', 2010, *Mail Online,* 1 November, dailymail.co.uk/sciencetech/article-1324882/Stone-Age-DIY-Cavemen-decorated-home-homemade-paint.html

Wikipedia.org/hand drums
Wikipedia.org/painting
Wikipedia.org/prehistoric-instruments

Chapter Four: Retreats

Beyond the Threshold: Vision Fast Australia, beyondthethreshold.net

Fogarty, Carole, *Rejuvenation Lounge,* thehealthylivinglounge.com

School of Lost Borders (United States): schooloflostborders.org

Stave, Rosie, *The Work of Byron Katie with Rosie,* theworkwithrosie.com

The Gawler Foundation, Melbourne Australia: gawler.org

The Work of Byron Katie, thework.com

Beyond the Threshold: Vision Fast Australia: beyondthethreshold.net

Vipassana Buddhist retreats – worldwide.

The Legal Stuff

About the author

Claire Bell has degrees in Arts and Education. She is a
qualified teacher, massage therapist and certified yoga
instructor. She is currently the health and wellbeing
editor of Midlifexpress, a news and information blog
for women based on the archetypes of midlife. She lives
in Melbourne, Australia, with her family.

www.ingramcontent.com/pod-product-compliance
Lightning Source LLC
Chambersburg PA
CBHW070521030426

42337CB00016B/2054